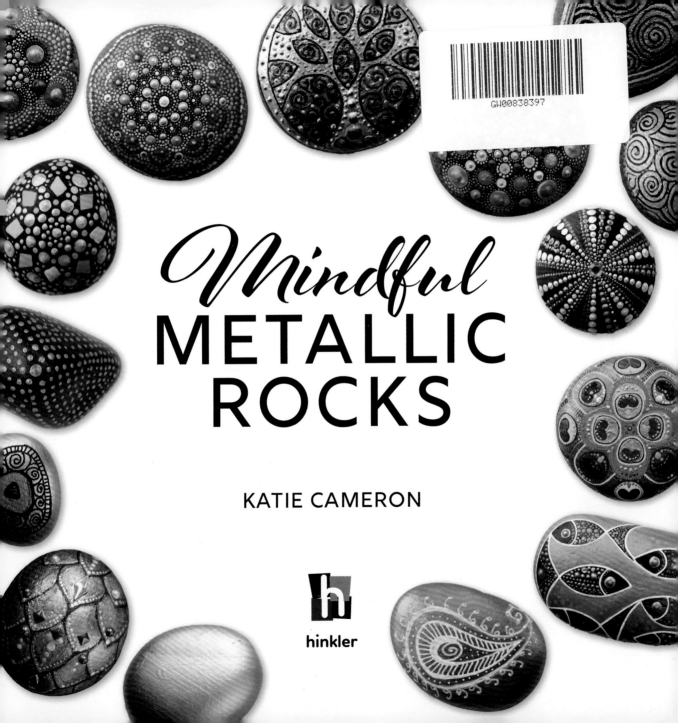

Mindful METALLIC ROCKS

KATIE CAMERON

hinkler

Mindful Metallic Rocks

Want to feel calm, happy, and centered? The simple act of holding a river stone in your hand, closing your eyes, and taking a few deep breaths is a swift and serene path to feeling connected with nature. Using metallic paint to decorate the river stone with mindful designs elevates it to an object that radiates with calm in its entirety—not only does the stone feel soothing, it is a pleasing and meditative point of visual focus.

In this book, you will learn a rewarding new pastime that will bring peace to your home or garden or bring positivity to a friend's life with a precious gift. There are eight mindful metallic rock-painting projects in this book, progressing from simple and charming through to intricate and sophisticated. Many of the designs draw on the natural world, taking their inspiration from the sea, land, sky, and beyond. There are even a few fantastical designs to help your imagination run wild!

You don't need to be a skilled painter to create these mindful artworks—with time, focus, and by simply following the steps, anyone can do it. Through the mindful art of rock painting, not only will you be communing with nature, you will be untapping the creative energies that rest within all of us.

Contents

Getting Started

First, let's look at some essential tips and tricks to get you started on your metallic rock-painting journey.

STONES

The best kind of stones to paint on are smooth and free of cracks or holes. If a stone has a bumpy surface, painting can be problematic and clean-line details are difficult to achieve. On top of that, metallic paint is especially unforgiving when it comes to uneven rock surfaces, revealing and even highlighting any dust, holes, or other imperfections that you may not have noted beforehand.

If you are going to gather your own stones, smooth stones are most commonly found along the shores of oceans and fast-moving rivers. If this is not an option, or if you want to save time, smooth stones can also be purchased from craft stores. Keep in mind that the larger the stone, the longer it can take to complete.

> IMPORTANT: *Make sure it's OK to take the stones from your area. Some places have regulations to protect the environment against things such as erosion or risks to animal habitat, and in some places it can be culturally inappropriate to remove stones. Ensure that you always ask permission if taking from private property.*

Be sure to thoroughly clean all your rocks before you start. Rinse off the bulk of any mud or sand outside (not down the kitchen drain, or it can get blocked), and then give them a scrub in the sink with soap and water. Leave them to air dry in a sunny location, such as a windowsill. Ensure the stones are free from any dust or debris and are completely dry before you begin.

PAINTS

Acrylic craft paint works very well for painting stones. It is non-toxic, fast drying, and adheres well to a stone's surface. It is affordable, easy to clean up, and simple to remove from brushes with a little soap and water.

Metallic acrylic craft paints share the same great qualities as regular craft paint and are a great addition to your art supplies. With metallic, you can add a delightful shimmer to just about all your craft or home décor projects. It is especially fabulous when painting on stone because, just like regular paint, it dries quickly and has good coverage. Metallic acrylic craft paint is water-based, making clean-up easy with a little soap and water. It is durable, and will keep its shine even if used with outdoor crafts.

Drying time can range from less than 5 minutes up to 15 minutes, or more. This is affected by several factors, including how thickly the paint is applied, temperature, and humidity. It can take up to 24 hours for acrylic paint to "cure" to the point that it is completely dry and at maximum hardness. It's important not to touch the stone during this time or you risk smudging it or leaving fingerprints. These are especially cumbersome to fix with metallic paint because its gleam attracts attention.

MIXING COLORS

You can easily create new color combinations with most acrylic paints, metallic included. Mix paints in a small container to make new colors; add a little bit of black to colors to create darker shades or add white to lighten them.

With metallic paints, you can mix them together to create some fun new colors or mix metallic with regular paint for a shiny new shade. Some combinations of metallic mix-ups are

gold + metallic blue = golden green
gold + metallic purple = rose gold
silver + gold = bronze
red + gold = copper

plus many more dazzling combinations!

If you find yourself without a color of metallic paint that you really need, you can actually make your own metallic paint colors by adding silver or white pearl paint (or mica-based eyeshadow since many metallic paints get their shine from the mineral mica!) to a regular matte shade you have on hand.

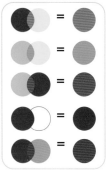

It's best to experiment with any DIY metallic paint mix-ups and "hacks" before beginning painting on stone.

METALLIC PAINTS

Metallic paints can either be sheer, semi-opaque, or opaque and it's important to know the coverage differences and the sorts of effects that you can create with each. Sheer paints are not meant to be used as a solid coat finish as they are translucent and used to create a sheen over another base paint. Metallic paint is typically opaque and takes 1–2 coats for best coverage. A "semi-opaque" paint requires 3 coats.

You can reduce the need for many coats of paint by first painting your stone with a primer, usually white or another light color that is similar to the metallic paint you are using. For example, use yellow paint to prime under gold metallic paint.

Painting with metallics is much the same as with regular paint, but there are a few differences you'll want to keep in mind. One problem you may run into is your brush strokes showing up visibly on your design, which is due to the shiny mineral pigment that metallic paint is made from. A stroke that is made from the left to the right can look different to a stroke that is made from right to left, so make your stone look more consistent by always painting in the same direction. Don't overload the paint on your soft-bristled brush or press down too hard on your brush while painting with metallic paints. Paint your details first then smooth over with any further coats. Apply thin coats and reload your brush often. Try to work quickly, if possible, painting in shorter strokes. Then go back and lightly drag the brush from one end of the stone to the other, always in the same direction. This will smooth out lines while you paint.

You may find that your stones develop ridges in your once-smooth painted surface. This is usually because there wasn't sufficient time for the first coat to dry before adding the next. The new coat pulled the layer below that wasn't quite dry along with it and no amount of additional coats will get you out of that mess. To fix this, it's best to make sure you allow the paint to fully dry, then use a fine sandpaper to sand down the bumps. Wipe away the dust and start again.

TOOLS

There are a few tools that are useful when designing and painting rocks:

- Pencil and eraser—use these to sketch out ideas and designs. Pencils can be used directly on the stone or on dry paint. Use an eraser to remove light markings when you're finished with them, or just paint over them.

- Drawing compass and ruler—you can use your eye to judge measurements, like center points or circles, but a ruler and compass make this faster and more accurate. These tools can help with guidelines used for hand-lettering spacing and proportions.

- Dotting tools—you can use wooden dowels, small round brushes, or you can make your own using an array of common household items. Needles, toothpicks, skewers, pencil ends: if it has a pointed tip, you can use it to paint dots. These rigid items allow more precision and control than a brush. A dotting stylus—also known as a nail-dotting tool or embosser—is a handy device that can be found at craft stores, is inexpensive, and works well for dotting with acrylic paint.

- Synthetic brushes—pointed and "detail round" brushes are best for fine detailing, dotting, and touch-ups. Thin brushes with long soft bristles are useful when painting longer outlines. Use a larger-sized round or flat brush when painting areas that need more coverage, like thick lines, primer, and base coats. The softness of your brush bristles, the amount of paint you have on the end, and how much pressure you use will also affect how paint is distributed

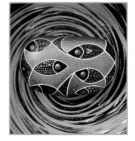

on the stone. Maintain brushes in good condition, keeping the bristles straight and together. Never let them dry with paint on. Only dip them into paint to about half the bristle length to avoid paint getting on the ferrule (the little metal piece attaching the bristles to the handle), which can result in fraying. A frayed brush will cause uneven dots, lines, or paint. Keep a cup of water at your work station so you can quickly swish off paint from brushes after use, lay them on a damp paper towel and thoroughly clean them when you are finished using them.

CLEAR FINISH

A protective finishing varnish can save time and preserve your art. Available at craft or hardware stores, it is quick and easy to use and adheres to all parts of the stone evenly. Choose the matte style to help prevent light reflection created by some paints. I prefer to use the spray-on type instead of a brush-on application, so I do not need to touch (and potentially smudge) the stone, in case it isn't completely dry or causes a reaction.

Finishing spray has many uses. Complete your artwork in less time by spraying it and allowing it to dry at key points in the process, so you can handle your stone between applying coats of paint. To prevent pencil mixing with white primer paint, spray clear finish over the pencil and allow it to dry before painting. A final coating when your art is complete will protect against fading and make it resistant against water and weather.

Spray your finish in a well-ventilated room or outside. Allow your stone to sit for at least a day for the finish and the art to dry entirely.

Some paints, permanent markers/pens, and gel pens can blur or smear when finishes are applied. Be sure to test how any materials you are using on your stones work with varnish BEFORE using them on your actual stone, such as on paper. Then do a test stone by covering it with those materials. Test the spray when your paint or ink is still damp as well as when it is completely dry. If the paint or ink reacts with the finish, it will blur into the colors around it. If this happens, use a different type of finish or consider other pens and paints.

OTHER TIPS AND TRICKS

PLAN AHEAD

Sketch out your design idea before you start. Trace the shape of your stone onto a piece of paper so you can get an idea of what will fit on your "canvas." Use a ruler and drawing compass to practice making circles and other geometric shapes. It's helpful to get the hang of a pattern on paper before it's set in stone.

PATIENCE

Painted stones can take many hours, if not days, to complete. Patience is key. If you rush, you may make mistakes that could have been avoided. That being said, don't worry too much about tiny paint imperfections. Often in the grand scheme of things they go unnoticed with all the other details around them and make your rocks unique.

PRACTICE

As with any craft, it takes practice to get results. Become familiar with how to use your brushes, dotting tools, or pens to get the best outcomes. Different brush sizes and shapes help achieve different paint strokes. Use a larger flat brush to cover large areas and smaller round brushes for details and outlines. Keep brush direction, angle, and pressure in mind when practicing. Use "practice rocks" to test out dots, paint lines, shades, and patterns to see what works.

A STEADY HAND

You need a relatively steady hand to apply paints precisely, and there are things you can do to help your hand stay smooth and stable. Keep the area of the stone you are working on directly in front of you and turn the stone as you go. Don't lift the stone: hold it still with one hand and anchor your other hand by placing your pinkie finger on the desk as you paint and draw.

When drawing, move your arm, not your wrist. Just remember, "pull curves and push straight." Your wrist naturally curves when it bends inward, so it feels more natural to "pull" down curves toward you and to "push" up away from you for straight lines. Paints and inks have varying degrees of thickness and consistency and the surface of your stone also factors into how you use your tools. You also may need to compensate for tiny holes or other imperfections.

Try to be focused, relaxed, and, if possible, uninterrupted when you work. Control your breathing: don't hold it. Take a deep breath before moments that require the utmost precision.

BLOCKING

Use masking tape to block off areas that you don't want to paint. Create crisp, clean paint lines and stripes using tapes of different widths. Make your own thin strips of masking tape with a utility knife. Layer 5 or 6 strips of tape on top of each other on a cutting board. Use a utility knife to slice the tape into thin strips that you can peel off for individual use. Firmly press the strips where you want the lines to be on the stone, then paint over them with 1–2 coats. Allow it to dry, then carefully peel off the tape.

Be careful of painting too many coats when masking, as this could result in thick ridges of paint along the edges or, worse, the paint coming up along with the tape removal.

PAINTING DOTS

Some of the designs in this kit involve applying dots. It's easiest to use a variety of dotting tools with different sized tips to get the size of dot you want. Hold the dotting tool in one hand as you would a pencil and, if needed, steady the rock with your other hand. If this is your first time creating dot art, try to hold the tool vertically to the stone, coming in at a 90-degree angle when applying dots. Steady your aim by resting your hand, wrist, or elbow against the desk or the stone itself. Once you become more accustomed to the way the paint transfers to stone, you will likely develop a method that's most comfortable for you.

To increase the size of each dot from one row to the next is mostly a matter of having the right amount of paint on the correctly sized stick. Usually the smaller the point, the smaller the dot will be. I often use the small pointed end of a toothpick and have gone so far as using a sewing needle for the most intricate dots. You can fashion your own needle tool by sticking the eye of the needle into the eraser of a pencil (as far as it will allow)—it is then much easier to hold on to. Other ways to achieve tiny dots would be to use the very tip of the longest bristle in a round paintbrush. You can always sharpen one end of your dotting tool to make it a smaller point.

When you want to go up in the size of a dot, you can use the same size dotting tool saturated in slightly more paint and add just a bit more pressure when touching the stick to stone. If you do not wipe the paint from the stick before re-dipping, it will start to dry and accumulate, enlarging the end of the tool. A bigger tool end will also give a bigger size dot.

ERASING MISTAKES

Oops! We all make mistakes, but mistakes can be fixed or avoided with a little planning. Many acrylic paint and gel-pen colors are opaque enough to paint over other colors and backgrounds without them showing through. This is what makes the base color your friend! Use it as an "eraser" for small mistakes. For wet paint or ink mistakes, wipe them away with water and a brush or cotton swab. If paint is dry, try lightly scraping the mistake off with fine sandpaper or an old emery board, then clear away any dust before painting the area with the underlying base-coat color. Good as new!

WORK SPACE

You will need a large, well-lit work space with enough room for you to paint in and that also has everything you need within arm's reach. Your station should be high enough to maintain good posture and be equipped with a comfortable chair.

To keep your work space neat and tidy, place a piece of cardboard or paper towel beneath your stone before you begin, and protect the remainder of your space with a drop-cloth or old newspaper. The cardboard helps keep the underside of the stone clean and can also be useful if you wish to move the stone to another area to dry.

What can you do with your stones after you paint them? Social media is a fantastic way to share your stunning metallic stones. It's an effective sharing tool that inspires people to create their own stone art. Fellow rock-painters can come together in community forums or on individual or group pages to share photos of their artwork.

HANDY HINT

Painting stones can take some time, so be aware of the time you're spending and try not to sit for too long! Get up, stretch, and move around for ten minutes or so at least once an hour. Movement is good for your body's circulation and can also help you refocus on the rock at hand.

Sharing Your Stones

There has been a huge rise in popularity of hide-and-seek-type games with painted rocks. Stones are painted then left in public spaces to be found. The rock "dropper" does not usually know who will find the stone, but knowing that someone will find the stone and that it will hopefully make them smile is enough to create those happy feelings that come with performing small acts of kindness.

The underside of the stone can have a web address or hashtag on it for further information. The person who discovers it can follow the web address or hashtag, which typically takes them to a website where the purpose and intent of the message is explained further. Besides the primary motive of brightening someone's day, the finder is often encouraged to take a photo of the stone themselves and post it online using the same hashtag, so everyone can share the artwork, see where it was discovered, and by whom.

If they like, the finder can keep the stone, though it is in the spirit of the movement to then hide a replacement painted rock of their own, which can bring joy to someone else's day. Alternatively, they hide the found stone in a new location. Anyone and everyone can join in! A person doesn't need to find a painted rock or be a member of a group to paint their own rocks for hiding. Start your own webpage featuring your art, invent a unique tag that links to your page, and use it on your stones that you leave out to be found. Follow other inspiring accounts of rock painters on social media to bring you further joy and to spark more creative ideas.

When hiding your rocks, ensure that it is in a public space that allows this activity. Popular places to hide rocks include parks, walking trails, and anywhere outdoors that is free for public use. Some places, such as national parks, prohibit taking or leaving stones, so it's best to check their guidelines first. Never hide your stones on private property without explicit permission.

A Journey of Discovery

Now that we have discussed the fundamentals, it's time to start painting! Every new pastime has a steep learning curve, which can be positively framed as a welcome journey of discovery. As you paint your stones, always center your thoughts and take your time. By being patient, foremost, you will stay focused. With this approach, you will feel rewarded by both the process and the marvelous eight rock artworks that result!

Shining Bubbles

Through a mindful and considered use of the brush, this very simple project depicts bubbles floating on a gentle breeze. Notice the curve of the bubbles' path and how each dot works in harmony with its neighbor for a showstopping effect.

YOU WILL NEED:

- 3 (or more) small, flat pebble-size stones. Preferably stones that "fit" well together and have close to the same thickness. These little stones are between 0.8–1.6 (2–4 cm) wide and they are quite flat, no more than 0.2 in (5 mm) thick.

- Paintbrush: small

- Dot tools: small, medium, large

- Paint: dark blue

- Metallic paint: silver, blue, gold, copper, purple

- Protective finish

1 Use your paintbrush to cover all 3 pebbles with dark blue paint. Arrange your stones so that they best "fit" together with as little space between where they touch as possible. Allow the paint to dry and paint another coat for best coverage.

2 When the paint is dry, take your small dotting tool and create a single winding line of small (0.07 in–2 mm) silver dots that curve from one stone to the next. Try to keep the stones together in their arranged placement while you paint.

3 Once you have the first line of silver dots, continue to build it thicker in some places (create more silver dots in the downward curves than the upward) using small, medium, and large dotting tools. Try to keep the dots very close together, but not touching.

4 With your metallic blue paint, dot small and medium sized dots beginning above the silver dots on the left stone. As you move across the stones, dot alongside the silver dotted line, then flip to the opposite side of the silver dots when you reach a curving "thin" area with fewer dots and continue on.

5 Follow the same dotting pattern using gold paint, only this time begin dotting under the silver dots on the left stone. Again, flip to the opposite side at thin areas. The gold dots and the blue dots will always be on opposite sides of the silver.

6 Add a thin line (1–2 dots) of metallic copper dots alongside the gold dots; as well, add a single dotted line of tiny metallic purple dots along the outside of the blue metallic dots. When the dot paint has dried, go back over them adding second coats. Use the base color dark blue paint to "erase" any mistakes or dots that have run into each other. Allow to dry before re-dotting. Allow to dry and then coat with protective finish.

HANDY HINT

Acrylic paint dries fairly quickly, so keep your brush slightly damp to help prevent this while you're painting. Just make sure that the brush is not so wet that it drips or dilutes the paint color that you're applying.

Pretty Paisley

As a famous symbol of the 1960s and hippy counterculture, the intriguing design of the paisley is both meditative and mind expanding. With its roots in 18th century Indian and Persian textiles, the paisley's interlocking curves look like an ornamental teardrop.

YOU WILL NEED:

- Oval-shaped stone approximately 2.7 in x 1.5 in (7 cm x 4 cm)
- Pencil
- Black permanent marker with extra-fine tip
- Metallic paint: gold, blue, purple
- Paintbrush: small
- Dotting tools: small
- Protective finish

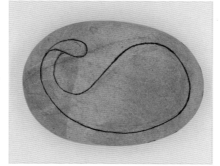

1 Draw the outline of a teardrop shape on the stone using pencil. When you're happy with it, go over it with black permanent marker.

2 Add the details inside the teardrop using a pencil, then trace over them with the black marker.

3 Using a black extra-fine-tipped permanent marker, draw the outline of a pointed fringe around the teardrop design. Then paint inside each shape with metallic gold and a small brush. Paint other sections of the design using gold, too.

4 Using a small brush, fill in more of the design with metallic blue paint, followed by metallic purple paint. When the paint has dried, add several additional coats, allowing the paint to dry in between layers. Touch up the black lines with a marker as you go.

5 Add the final, pretty paisley details, such as clusters of gold dots around the outside, contrasting colored dots and lines within the design, and a final touch-up wherever needed. When the paint is dry, coat the stone with protective finish.

HANDY HINT

Layering paint strategically can produce some really neat texture to the art once the stone is dry and the paint has cured. Adding more layers of one color than the others will make that part of the painted stone puff out, and adding extra layers of dots or lines will create bumps and ridges so that when handled, the stone is amazing to both see and touch!

Dragon Egg

As a symbol of renewal, the Dragon Egg is a celebration of folklores and mythologies from around the world. As you paint each shimmering scale, try recalling and meditating upon your own childhood wonder at stories of dragons and faraway kingdoms!

YOU WILL NEED:

- Oval or egg-shaped stone (2.5 in or 6 cm length)
- Pencil
- Fine-tip black permanent marker (or black paint)
- Paint: gray, black (optional)
- Metallic paint: green, dark green, blue, purple, gold
- Paintbrush: small, medium
- Dotting tools: small, medium, large
- Protective finish
- Small gems and adhesive (optional)

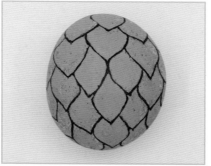

1 Paint the stone with a light-colored base (I have used gray paint). This means you'll need fewer coats of metallic paint. Using a fine-tip black marker or black paint and a small brush, draw rows of pointed scales to cover the stone from top to bottom. Make sure the scales are of an equal size.

2 Paint the entire stone with metallic green paint. (If you don't have green, you can mix gold and blue metallic paint). Refresh the black scale outline if needed.

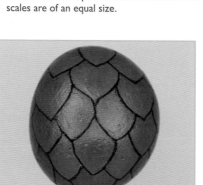

3 Use a different shade of metallic green to add shading along the edges and corners of the scales where they overlap.

4 When the paint is dry, use a smaller brush to paint contrasting colors through the middle of each of the scales. Paint metallic blue through the center scales and metallic purple in the side scales. Leave a border of green along the edge of each scale. Once the paint has dried, paint a second coat and blend more into the green borders.

6 Apply any additional gems or other mixed media once the stone has completely dried. Using tweezers helps to place them on the stone.

5 Refresh the black outlines around the scales and add decorative detailing: paint small gold dots along the edges of the scales and a line of larger dots running down the center of the stone. Remember to leave room if you plan to use gems or other ornaments. Spray your stone with protective finish.

HANDY HINT

Decorate the egg with gemstones or other metallic decorative beads or sequins. Just remember to wait until after the stone has been coated with protective finish before gluing anything to the stone. Try using other mixed media to decorate the stone: you could use a hot glue gun on the stone and then paint over the glue when dry.

 # Fish Flow

Ideal for Pisceans, try carrying this little oasis of calm in your pocket as a mindful reminder to relax and "go with the flow." The soothing color palette and pattern will help you imagine the peaceful ambience of a real creek or river.

YOU WILL NEED:

- Stone (roughly 4 in x 2.5 in (10 cm x 6 cm), but this design can be adapted to fit on just about any shape or size of stone)

- Paint: silver or gray, white, dark blue, dark green, dark purple, gold

- Metallic paint: green, blue, dark blue, purple, dark green, turquoise, light purple, white

- Paintbrush: small, medium, large

- Dotting tools: small, medium

- Protective finish

1 Draw a fish pattern outline on the stone in pencil, then trace over it with white paint. Paint the surrounding "water" area with a silver or gray base coat.

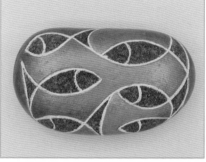

2 When the base coat is dry, paint the next coat using metallic green in the middle and metallic blue toward the outside edges. Paint a darker shade of blue at the bottom edges of the stone for deeper water and a more golden green to light blue at the top.

3 While the "water" dries, paint inside the white lines of the fish with dark blue matte paint. At the same time, use the dark blue to shape the white lines so they are all the same thickness (0.4–0.8 in or 1–2 mm). Add additional coats of "water" on the other side of the white lines to also shape them.

4 Paint dots inside the fish with small and medium dotting tools using dark shades of green, blue, and purple matte paint. Use a large dotting tool to add big silver dots for eyes.

5 When the paint has dried, add small dots on top of the large dots using metallic paint of a similar but lighter color. Dot the eyes with metallic turquoise, then metallic blue, then a tiny white metallic pearl dot in the center.

6 Add any final dots, bubbles, and touch-ups, such as gold dots on the green areas and rows of small white dots where desired. Spray with protective finish.

HANDY HINT

A white gel pen can be helpful to make minor touch-ups to the white lines. If you don't have a white pen, try using tape to mask areas where you're painting to make straight lines.

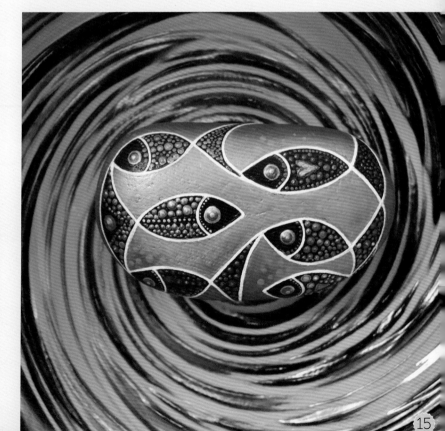

Cosmic Tree

As a universal symbol, the Cosmic Tree inspires reflection and deep thought. Occurring in different cultures across the world, the tree reminds us of our place in nature. The Cosmic Tree encourages us to be mindful and grounded, with its roots plunging deep into the earth.

YOU WILL NEED:

- Flat, round stone (approximately 2.5 in (6 cm) in diameter)
- Pencil
- Black fine-tip marker (optional)
- Paint: black
- Metallic paint: teal blue, purple, silver, gold
- Paintbrush: small, medium
- Dotting tools: small, medium
- Protective finish

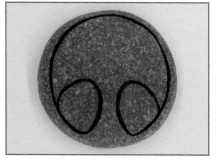

1 Using a pencil, draw a circle around the edge of the stone, but don't close it up: leave a 1 in (2.5 cm) space at the bottom and continue the lines up into the circle and away from the center, stopping at the circle line. You should have two symmetrical oval shapes. This makes up the trunk of the tree. Trace over your pencil lines with a thin black marker.

2 Fill in the rest of the tree's branches by adding small leaf shapes through the center of the circle and symmetrically along both sides. Lightly form a full circle to make a border around the entire design at about 0.2–0.4 in (0.5–1 cm) from the stone's edge. Trace the shapes with black marker.

3 Paint the leaf shapes with metallic teal blue paint. Allow to dry, then paint another coat for extra coverage.

4 When the shapes are completely dry, use a pencil to draw swirling lines throughout each, then trace over these swirls with metallic purple paint using a small brush (please see the "Handy Hint" on the next page).

It can be difficult to clearly see your work with such metallic paints shining in your eyes. If you find this happening, tilt the stone in various directions until you find a spot where the glare is out of your eyes and you can clearly see your detailed handiwork.

5 Use a small brush to paint the entire tree with metallic silver paint. When the first coat has dried, add another coat and use a small dotting tool to dot small silver dots throughout the tree branches. Allow to dry. Use silver paint and a fine-tipped black marker to even up the lines and do touch-ups along the branches.

6 Paint silver around the outside of the circle and fill in the border. When the paint is dry, trace over the line edges with black marker. Add the final small silver dots around the border and in the trunk, as well as gold star dots in the blue and purple sky. Leave to dry.

7 When the paint has dried, paint the outer edges of the stone purple. Paint the larger silver dots in the trunk. Add any final coats of color and outlines, allow to dry, then coat with protective spray.

Golden Pyramid

Since antiquity, the pyramid has been a symbol of grounded foundations with the pointed top representing a journey toward the higher realms of consciousness. Meditate upon this symmetrical rock art design with its pools of gold radiating a primordial strength and power!

YOU WILL NEED:

- Round stone (about 2.5 in (6 cm) in diameter)
- Pencil
- Compass
- Paint: black, yellow, gold, pearl white, orange, red, bright red
- Metallic paint: blue, light yellow, purple
- Paintbrush: small, medium
- Dotting tools: small, medium, large
- Protective finish

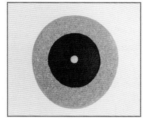

1 Form a large, 1 in (3 cm) dot that takes up about half of the space in the center of the stone. Fill the circle with black paint using a medium brush. When the paint has dried, use a medium-sized dotting tool and metallic blue paint to add a 0.2 in (5 mm) dot in the center of the black circle.

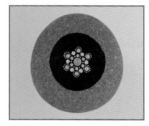

2 Use a small dotting tool and bright yellow paint to evenly place six small dots of equal size about 0.6 in (1.5 cm) around the blue center icon. On a clock, these would be at 12, 2, 4, 6, 8 and 10 o'clock. Carefully add 0.4 in (1 cm) or smaller dots of metallic blue between each of the bright yellow dots. Try to make sure you don't touch any of the existing dots as you make more dots. Continue to move out from the center icon. Place another ring of six metallic light-yellow dots that are 0.8 in (2 cm): just slightly larger than the bright yellow dots in the previous ring. Add some tiny blue dots between them.

3 For the dots in the next ring, make them the same size but use gold paint. Place these gold dots in line with the bright yellow dots. Leave a bit more space between the gold dots and those around them so that you can add a ring of tiny 0.2 in (0.5 cm) metallic pearl white dots around each of the gold dots individually.

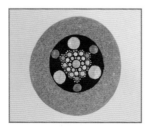

4 At 12, 4, and 8 on a clock, add two tiny dots of bright orange, side by side. In the remaining three spaces, add small bright orange dots, spacing them so that you can fit a ring of tiny gold dots around each. The dots should combine to form a triangular shape. Use a large dotting tool to make three large 0.3 in (8 mm) dots of gold just above the two small orange dots. Make these gold dots large enough to just touch the edge of the black circle. Add three medium size 0.2 in (5 mm) metallic purple dots in line with the gold-circled bright orange dots.

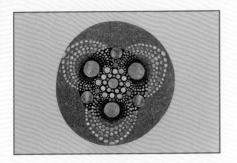

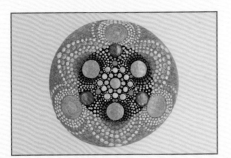

5 Focus your attention on the large gold dots. Begin to add rings of dots that slightly increase in size with each new ring. The first ring is made of tiny red dots, followed by bright red, bright orange, bright yellow, metallic pastel yellow, gold, and finally metallic white pearl. As you add the rings, you will need to slightly reduce the size of the dots. Add a couple of metallic blue dots to fill in the corners next to the metallic purple dots.

6 Use a small paintbrush to make three extra-large 0.4 in (1 cm) gold dots in line with the metallic purple dots. Add rings of tiny dots of yellow, gold, and metallic white pearl. These rings should wrap around the side of the stone.

HANDY HINT

Mix and mingle! Use different types of paint such as matte and neon in your designs and highlight them using shimmering metallics.

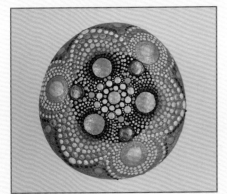

7 Add metallic blue dots in the corners where the white pearl dots meet. Create a ring of small metallic purple dots surrounding the entire design. Add finishing touches, like a second coat of paint anywhere that it is needed. When all is dry, add 1–2 coats of protective finish.

Proud Peacock Mandala

Draw upon this peacock mandala in meditation for its symbols of nobility, guidance, protection, and watchfulness. The peacock and its stunning display of vibrant feathers can help you feel revitalized and, when blocked or inhibited, encourage you to reveal your true colors.

YOU WILL NEED:

- Large stone, either round or square (about 4 in (10 cm) in diameter)
- Pencil
- Ruler
- Paint: dark navy blue, green, turquoise, gold, bronze, purple
- Metallic paint: golden green, turquoise blue, purple, blue, pink, dark green
- Paintbrush: small, medium, large
- Dotting tools: small, medium
- Black extra-fine tip permanent pen
- Protective finish

1 Use a pencil and ruler to draw a 3 × 3 in (75 × 75 mm) square or diamond shape across the top of the stone. Use a large brush to fill the square with dark blue paint. When the paint is dry, use your pencil to draw two more squares sized 2 × 2 in (50 × 50 mm) and 1.5 × 1.5 in (38 × 38 mm) within the first square. You can lightly draw horizontal, vertical, and diagonal lines through the center of the large square to help place the other squares inside, as well as to divide the squares into four: each of these sections will become a peacock feather "eye." Roughly outline the medium square with green and the small square with turquoise paint.

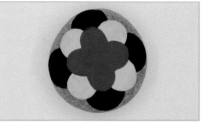

2 Fill each of the small center squares with matte turquoise-blue paint. As you paint around the points and edges of each square, extend them into the next square. Shape them approximately 0.2 in (5 mm) larger than their original size. Allow to dry, then do the same for the next square: fill it with matte green paint and round the edges, and extending it out slightly and into the currently bare stone. Finally, round the edges of the dark blue square. Ensure that all squares (or feathers) are about the same size and shape; it should resemble a stack of four-leaf clovers.

3 When the paint is dry, add additional coats for solid coverage. Paint over the green section with metallic golden-green paint. With your pencil, lightly add the details of the peacock feathers in the turquoise section. For each feather, draw an oval that almost fills the shape, leaving about 0.7–1.5 in (2–4 cm) of a border. Inside this, draw another smaller oval with a slightly flattened top. Using gold, paint the first oval outline in the small center feathers.

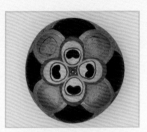

4 While the gold paint dries, continue painting the rest of the feathers. Within the flat-topped oval, draw a short, wide heart shape, closer to the flat top. Make the heart upside down, so its base points out to the edge of the stone. This is the pattern for all feathers: you can modify it to fit each section area. Begin to paint the rest of the colors, layering the colors and allowing them to dry in between. Allow time for each new section you've painted to dry before moving on to the next. Paint the remaining center feathers metallic turquoise blue with a matte turquoise border line left showing and dark navy blue for the hearts. Color the middle section of feathers bronze, then metallic purple.

5 While the paint dries, add contrasting colored border lines around the ovals where the paint is already dry. Paint a bright lime-green border around the bronze oval and another around the metallic blue oval in the center section. For the largest section of feathers, the outer-most ovals, the first oval is painted metallic blue.

6 Once the paint has dried, paint a matte bright lime-green circle inside the metallic blue in the large section. Add purple hearts inside the metallic purple middle section of feathers. Go around the outside of the middle section with navy blue border lines.

7 Paint metallic pink hearts in the green oval of the large outer feathers. Add purple borders around the ovals in the middle and outer sections and refresh any colored border lines that need it.

8 When the paint is all dry, go over the design to add details. Add small metallic dark green dots around the golden green oval and small lines with black pen inside the golden green of the mid-feathers. Draw medium-sized gold dots along the outside edge of the mid-feathers, small dots of matte green in the navy border of the large feathers, and small gold dots around the matte turquoise center feathers. Add dots of different colors inside the hearts. When the paint is dry, coat the stone with protective spray.

HANDY HINT

Make your own golden peacock-green metallic paint by mixing metallic blue and gold paint together. Make this and any other new paint colors before beginning so that they are ready to use when the time comes. Store in a small, air-tight container to keep them from drying out.

Enchanted Urchin Amulet

With its spiral motif, the Enchanted Urchin Amulet will draw you in to a mesmerizing feeling of ocean calm. With simple shading, the rock's metallic colors glisten and shimmer as though they are waves, providing a freshness and serenity to every moment.

YOU WILL NEED:

- Small round stone — 2 in (5 cm)
- Paint: navy, violet, metallic white pearl
- Metallic paint: blue, gold, purple, rose gold
- Paintbrush: small, medium
- Dotting tools: small, medium, large
- Protective finish

1 Paint the base coat with matte navy and matte violet. Paint the colors in alternating star shapes with five-part symmetry.

2 Use a large dotting tool and white pearl paint to make a 0.1 in (3–4 mm) dot in the center of the stone; use a small dotting tool to make 10 tiny dots around the large one. Try to keep them all the same size (0.04 in/1 mm) and line them up with the edges where one base color meets the next.

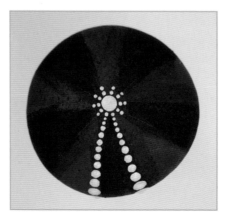

3 Continue to use white pearl paint and begin to add small dots in line with the center dots that span out to the edge of the stone. Increase the size of the dots as they move outward so that the dots on the edge of the stone are as large as the center icon.

4 Use a small dotting tool to make more lines of dots that span out from the center icon. Create lines of small metallic blue dots after every second pearl line. Unlike the pearl white dots, keep your metallic blue dots tiny all the way to the outer edge of the stone.

5 Add 5 lines of gold medium-size dots 0.08 in (2 mm) down the middle of each violet base color. The gold dots should get slightly larger as they move out from the middle of the rock.

6 Continue adding lines of colored dots that span out from the center icon. As the available space begins to fill up, taper the dots closest to the center icon and increase their size (if desired) as you span toward the stone's edge. Add rows of purple dots and rows of dots of rose gold (formed by mixing metallic purple and gold). Next to the existing rows of gold dots, add lines made up of small metallic blue and tiny gold dots.

7 Make any final touch-ups and when the stone has dried, cover with protective finish. If adding a gem in the center for some extra sparkle, apply it once the finish has been applied and is dry.

HANDY HINT

If you are using a gemstone in the center of the urchin, make sure that your first center dot is about the same size as the gem you will use. If it's too large, it will show under the gem and if it's too small, you will be cutting off the dots that surround the center when the gem is applied at the very end.

Congratulations!

Wow, you have taken the time to really connect with the art of rock painting and choose a path of mindful serenity in the process. What will you do with your meditative mindful rock art creations now?

A very natural decision would be to gift your mindful metallic rock art to friends and family. Be sure to provide a little backstory about your journey with the rock art, and what each painted design represents. You might suggest that the lucky person who receives the rock uses it as an aid to meditate and be mindful, too!

One of the most wonderful things about finding joy in a new hobby is inspiring others to join you. While educating yourself on the art of rock painting has most likely been a solitary venture, why not share knowledge and work together with friends and family? Spread the word and form a group—or a "rock art band" for fun!

For every rock you create (either for yourself or to send out into the world), be sure to take a "shelfie"—that's a photo of a stone on a shelf where it can sit and pose with other treasures you may have among your décor. Of course, any setting that brings out the metallic sparkle will look great. On a windowsill, by a houseplant, or outdoors in the garden space, your precious metals will decorate with a glimmer of happiness wherever they are.

Get inspired and continue your stone art journey. You don't have to look far for ideas—inspiration is never more than a stone's throw away …

A Note on the Author

Katie Cameron lives and creates in Halifax, Nova Scotia, Canada's ocean playground. She is a self-taught rock artist and, when not creating home-made magic, she can be found strolling the coastline in search of the perfect stone for her next #HFXrocks creation.

Katie has released many painted rock tutorial kits since teaming up with Hinkler in 2015. You can find her other titles and more through hinkler.com.au. Keep shining and always think happy dots!